JACK ZARIA

MAKE BIG THINGS HAPPEN

The Ultimate Guide On How to Improve and Level Up Your Life, Know How to Increase Your Self-Confidence and Embrace Positivity to Make Great Things Happen

Descrierea CIP a Bibliotecii Naţionale a României
JACK ZARIA
MAKE BIG THINGS HAPPEN. The Ultimate Guide On How to Improve and Level Up Your Life, Know How to Increase Your Self-Confidence and Embrace Positivity to Make Great Things Happen / Jack Zaria – Bucharest: Editura My Ebook, 2021
ISBN

JACK ZARIA

MAKE BIG THINGS HAPPEN

The Ultimate Guide On How to Improve and Level Up Your Life, Know How to Increase Your Self-Confidence and Embrace Positivity to Make Great Things Happen

My Ebook Publishing House
Bucharest, 2021

TABLE OF CONTENTS

CHAPTER 1

TRANSFORM YOUR LIFE, NOW!

If you look at achievers and those who failed to "get there," you would see the former with a unique mindset – one that is molded out of confidence and optimism. This is what sets them apart from the rest as they have a positive outlook in life and a unique path set out for them as they take on life's journey.

But to start changing your life, you need to set your goals first. What would you like to become? What specific aspect in life should you address in order to make that dramatic transformation for the better?

For one, make sure to stay focused on your goals. That way, you can confidently make decisions that will change the direction of your life. Clear out any confusion. The idea of change can be quite scary that the thought of getting through a month, a week, or a day might prove to be a challenge.

However, you can take it one step at a time to avoid being overwhelmed.

It would help if you list down all the things that you want to do. This should make some things crystal clear for you in the midst of all the confusion in your mind. This will also help you see your priorities in black and white.

It does not even matter how you organize your list, just as long as you put your thoughts into writing. Once the list is done, give yourself some time to sort it through and identify the least to the most important things to do.

When you start setting goals, be realistic about it. Don't make it look like you're giving a genie three wishes, such as when you wish to become a millionaire overnight, because every impossible goal is a cause for disappointment and disillusionment. Just be grounded, focused, and realistic about your goals. There's nothing wrong with starting small.

It would be better if your first goal is achievable within a month or two, but it should still be significant enough to give you a great taste of success. Your next goal should be something connected to the realization of the first goal, and so on.

You may also set goals that aim to eliminate all the negative things in life that have kept you from succeeding. It could be to get rid of your inhibitions and self-limitations.

For many achievers, their first goal is to excel in time management. This is an appropriate first goal, especially for people who always seem to be running out of time. Proper time management will make you feel in control and confident that you can achieve your goals in time.

When creating your to-do list, you may also want to take note of the things that are hindering you from success. It could be your fear of failure, something that many people fail. In many cases, failure is usually about fears dominating your subconscious. So, what are you really afraid of?

As you choose your ultimate goal, do you still have doubts about your ability to realize it? If so, you need to get to the bottom of it all and discover where those doubts come from.

Everyone has fears, but you need to take it on if you want to leave the old you behind and move on to the new you. What is pulling you behind from transforming into the person that you want to become?

Aside from writing your goals, you need to be reminded of them at all times. Look at your list regularly make your visions of success clearer and stronger than ever.

You can be the new you by taking small but effective steps. Set your goals, follow them, create a course of action, and get rid of your self-doubts. Use your mental strength to put your positive thoughts at the center of everything that you are doing and relieve yourself of all the negative thoughts until you totally forget about them.

Monitor your progress and your timescales. Don't stray and follow your realistic deadlines. Careful tracking of your goals and your current actions will tell you if you are still on schedule or whether you need to pick up the pace to keep up with your deadlines. Every time you tick off a task on your to-do list, it can give you a different kind of satisfaction knowing that you're about to do something great! Don't be stingy in rewarding yourself.

As you are about to reach your goals, you will also feel your confidence and self-worth building up over time.

CHAPTER 2

MOTIVATION: HOW TO FIND AND KEEP IT

One of the most important steps towards changing yourself is to know what motivates you. Once you discover what drives you, you can use it to jumpstart everything that you need to do for a total transformation.

Know more about yourself by reflecting on your biggest achievement in life and what you did to realize it.

There are certain questions that will help you understand yourself more and your source of motivation.

Be honest in answering these questions and write them down for a better analysis later.

1. What do you consider as your greatest accomplishment in life so far?

2. What did you do to achieve it?

3. What drove you on to achieve your goal?

4. How did you continue to motivate yourself?

5. How much do you value your final goal?

After answering these questions, take the time to recall just how happy you felt during that moment when you knew that you finally achieved your goal.

Motivation differs from one person to the other. However, your dreams will likely remain the same over time.

In most cases though, people often choose to abandon their lofty dream and downgrade it to something that is easier to realize. However, settling for something less may not give you that sense of fulfillment knowing that it isn't your genuine dream in the first place.

But you can find a way to stop yourself from losing hope and motivation. It is to always keep in touch with the way you feel about your dreams and to remind yourself of those feelings, especially during an emotional crisis.

Use this list to understand your feelings about your dreams better:

❑ Do you want people to acknowledge you and your achievements?

❑ Do you want to help your family?

- Do you get your sense of personal satisfaction by proving that you are an important figure or that you can realize all your goals?
- Do you always stick to doing the right thing?
- Do you want to improve your financial status?
- Do you feel passionate about life and let it consume you?
- Did you have a difficult childhood, enough that you would not want to experience it again in adulthood?
- Do you always want to feel in control and do something that contributes to achieving your dreams?
- Do you handle changes positively?
- Do you feel even more determined to achieve your goals once you see them written down clearly as your priorities?

Many of these questions pertain to your feelings about your goals in life. Make sure to put these questions somewhere visible as a daily reminder of why you should continue pursuing your dreams no matter what. These should help you hold on to the motivated you!

CHAPTER 3

STOP PROCRASTINATING NOW!

Do you often catch yourself wasting time instead of spending it on tasks that matter? Do you always feel guilty when you can't catch up with deadlines or fail to finish anything of significance?

Although many people share this bad habit of procrastination, it doesn't mean that it is a habit worth continuing. You have to correct it as soon as you notice it, if you want to avoid disappointing yourself over and over again. The worst case scenario is when procrastination causes depression and lack of self-worth, as you see yourself wasting your time and your opportunities to succeed in life.

There might even be a time when getting started is a challenge in itself, but you need to change this behavior if you don't want to establish it as a habit that you can't abandon for life. You need to get yourself moving and get started on your to-do list.

If you find yourself procrastinating, then consider doing these things and making a habit out of them:

- ❑ **Manage your time better by starting your day with a to-do list.** Write down all the tasks that you want to finish for the day and arrange them by priority. It would be even better if you make your list the night before so you can get started on it first thing in the morning.

- ❑ **Get up early with an alarm.** Don't waste your time by procrastinating in bed because this can delay all the other tasks for the day and you'll end up chasing time. Being an hour ahead of your tasks can give you a sense of satisfaction rather than catching up with deadlines.

- ❑ **Break your tasks down into smaller tasks.** That way, you will avoid feeling overwhelmed about all the things that you need to do. Once you get that sense of satisfaction from accomplishing a small task or two, you will likely have the motivation to finish all your tasks for the day.

- **Learn to negotiate with yourself.** If you finish your tasks, you can go out with friends later, watch a movie with them, or reward yourself with a trip.

- **Don't spend too much time in front of the TV.** You might not notice how much time you waste on your favorite TV programs. Be picky in choosing your TV programs, or record them, and watch them only when you're done with your tasks. This might even serve as a good reward to get you through your tasks because you know that you can relax later.

- **Give yourself a break, especially when everyone has lazy days too!** However, don't overdo it. Instead, imagine how happy you'll feel once you reach your goals. Visualization is an effective tool to help replenish your energy and motivation to make your dream a reality.

- **Punish yourself with a consequence if you can't finish your tasks.** For instance, if you don't work out three times a week, you have to stay at home during the weekends.

- **Feed off on your fear to get you going. Fear is an intense emotion.** If you focus on the things that you don't want to happen, you can use it in your favor. Write down exactly what might happen or how you will feel if you fail to achieve your goals after a certain time. Be honest about what it would cost you if you continue doing nothing and failing.

- **Be accountable.** Find a support team or someone who will hold you accountable. Make time to check-in with them regularly and tell them what you are up to, where you are in your journey towards achieving your goals, and what your support team can do to help. They could help you recall about your past achievements or kick-start the changes that you need to do in life.

- **Be brave.** It is important that you build momentum when you start doing something. Starting today, stop making excuses and fight your laziness. You can start small, as long as it takes you forward towards the direction of achieving your goals. Take that first step, second step, and so on. Start now!

CHAPTER 4

INCREASE SELF-CONFIDENCE
AND BANISH SELF-DOUBT

Do you find your self-doubts distracting? Do you find yourself second guessing your actions and decisions, or even your achievements? If you don't address these self-doubts, these might accumulate to form negative thoughts about yourself that will ruin your confidence and self-esteem. The longer you leave them alone, the more they will feed on your sense of self- worth. Eventually, you will feel paralyzed about doing things for fear of failing.

It is always challenging to break that barrier of negativity once it has taken a strong hold in your life, but it is important that you remain strong and firm in turning it around and getting rid of your self-doubts. This is the only way for you to inject positivity in life.

Spend some time to address those doubts and understand why you feel that way about yourself. Get to the bottom of it all and you'll know how to regain your confidence. It usually starts when you handle a challenge way bigger than those you have seen before, leading to you questioning your ability to take it on.

If you keep telling yourself "I can't do this!" you might stop yourself from doing anything else because you're afraid to fail. However, you have to get on with life, take on challenges, and accept whatever happens. Most of all, you have to learn from all your successes and failures.

Learn to stop yourself from thinking negative thoughts before they even start paralyzing you from doing your tasks. Every time such thoughts pop up, squish them clean and replace them with the endless opportunities that are in store for you for the day. The quicker you do this, the better control you'll have over them. If you're in control, you will eventually boost your confidence and self-worth.

And when you do catch yourself thinking negatively, don't beat yourself up over it. Think about how long you have held onto this habit and how you can't get rid of it overnight.

Every time you notice your old behaviors coming back, correct it right away and give yourself a pat in the back. Being aware of your mistakes is the key step towards transforming

19

your life and changing your attitude towards it. You're halfway there!

It is not easy to be completely free of mistakes, but you can make the most out of every mistake by learning from it. Don't let your feelings of shame linger either. Give yourself a break. You're only human, after all.

When your guards are down and you start feeling those old doubts again, win those thoughts over with a positive attitude. For instance, instead of thinking "I'm not good enough for this job!" or "I don't do well in interviews," think "This job is a going to be a handful, but I can do it!" or "I'm going to do well during the interview and prove to them that I'm the person they're looking for the position."

It also helps to write down all the good things about you and remind yourself of such characteristics every time you feel down. You might be surprised at how many positive qualities you have more than the negative ones. Once you realize this, you will feel confident about yourself.

CHAPTER 5

THE POWER OF BEING POSITIVE

It is not easy to stay upbeat and positive at all times. However, you need that mindset as the basic requirement for transforming your life and being successful. There are some tips on how you can always maintain a positive disposition in life.

Focus On The Positive

This is the first thing that you need to do if you want to clear your mind of all negativities. Train it to see only the best in people and the good things in any situation.

However you perceive a situation affects your response. If the mind can process things positively, then it is likely that you will resolve any problem successfully as well.

Be With Positive People

Surround yourself with positive-minded people to help them feed your positivity towards life, too. Stay away from negative people to avoid being steered towards their direction. Make sure to stick only to doing positive things that will contribute to achieving your dreams.

Surround Yourself With Anything Positive

Aside from choosing the company of positive people, make everything around you positive as well. Make it so that you will hear positive audio, see positive posters and visuals, and learn of positive statements and quotes. You live by what you see, hear, or learn.

Exercise Regularly

It is scientifically proven that regular exercise can regulate the body's chemical balance, giving off positive energy, which in turn, sets a positive mindset for you.

Make time for exercise, even if it is just walking your dog around the block or playing with your kids in the park. Yoga and meditation can also help you maintain a positive mindset, aside from relieving stress that attracts negative energy.

How To Avoid Being Negative Thinkers

Negative self-talk will stop you from thinking positive. However, it is easier for people to think negatively that negative thoughts would likely come to mind faster than positive ones. Eventually, these people will feel insecure, indecisive, and excessively apologetic. They might even experience stress-related problems.

These negative thinkers usually have these mindsets:

- **Personalizing**. Some people attribute all the negative things that are happening to them to being unlucky. They keep blaming themselves for doing or not doing something, leading to various tragedies in life. Negative thinkers are often active in coming up with negative situations, finding reasons to blame themselves for those situations.

- **Filtering**. Negative thinkers often focus on the bad things in a situation. They refuse to see the positive side of things. Eventually, they make a habit out of it.

- **Polarizing**. This kind of mindset among negative thinkers makes them think that a situation is either perfect or catastrophic. This can ruin all the aspects of one's life, physically, emotionally, and psychologically.

- **Catastrophizing**. This is about thinking about the worst. There are negative thinkers who over think the worst case scenario in situations. If something bad happens, they even see it as a confirmation that their worst assumptions are coming true.

If you avoid these kinds of mindsets, you can save yourself from the stress that negative thinking brings and possibly avoid the medical condition that stress brings. It's time to start feeling positive and let it dominate your life. You can start with choosing the company of positive people.

Depression has mental and physical elements. Even a person with a positive outlook is not totally safe from depression.

However, that positive attitude towards life can help in treating depression. You can use it to stop yourself from going to over to the dark side completely. It can show you that life still has good things to offer and that you have a way out of your depression, especially if your positivity wins over your negative thinking habits.

Positive thinkers tend to show a lower incidence of medical conditions, especially cardiovascular diseases. They usually have lower blood pressure than negative thinkers. Optimists also tend to deal with stress better, leading to a better psychological and physical condition.

Being positive might not prevent bad things from occurring, but it can help you handle negative situations better. Feel it's real power now!.

CHAPTER 6

ATTRACT THE POSITIVE PEOPLE
INTO YOUR LIFE

If you felt like there's no way you could regain your confidence once more, it's time to start looking into your relationships and check what kind of people you have surrounded yourself with.

Hold onto genuine friends and find new friends who want to adapt the same positive mindset that you want to have. Try to let go of people who bring you down with their negative attitude.

But how would you know who are the positive people and who aren't?

Identifying Positive People

Positive people can be distinguished by these characteristics:

❑ They have courage to follow their dreams.

- They are compassionate towards others and themselves.
- They are ready to open their heart to other people.
- They know their negative characteristics and are willing to embrace and accept them.
- They learn from their mistakes.

On the other hand, you might not want to be associated with people who have the following characteristics, if you want to maintain positivity in life:

- They seem all too real about being positive and perfect all the time.
- They beat themselves over mistakes and other shortcomings.
- They do not pay that much attention to their well-being, which means you cannot exactly expect them to look after yours.
- They are dominated by their fear.
- They do not acknowledge their dark side, but take it out on other people.

How To Boost Your Positive Signals

If you want to attract positive people, you have to release good vibes by following these steps:

> ➤ **Understand the best things about you and project them to others**. Reflect on yourself and determine your finest qualities. It could be compassion, sensitivity, wit, and more. Share them to the world by speaking up and meeting people. Show those qualities actively and people will notice, especially those who share those very qualities with you.

> ➤ **Express love**. Learn to appreciate all the things that you love in the world. It could be the blue skies, the never-ending horizon, the babble of innocent children, the taste of your mom's cooking, and more. Love can attract positive people.

> ➤ **Meditate**. Make a habit out of anything positive, but to let those habits out, you need to meditate. Do it regularly and focus on all the positive emotions that you feel during the process. Eventually, your vibes will turn positive too.

➢ **Be more aware of yourself.** This is your greatest tool against fear and self-doubts. This will also stop you from being negative, so you can continue to reach out to positive people.

Remember that positivity begets positivity and it is an important element on your way to understanding yourself better and your transformation. This journey may not exactly be smooth, but you might be surprised just how tough you can be to weather even the roughest ride in life. Stay motivated by looking forward to all the opportunities that are in store for you once you complete your transformation.

You will be the one enjoying all the benefits of this change anyway, so it's going to be worth it. However, you can't make that change unless you stop doubting yourself and feel confident in your own skin.

As you are well on your way towards changing yourself for the better, even the smallest steps matter. Your transformation won't be complete without each single step. On that journey, expect to find people who think the way you do. As you befriend these people, it will create more positivity in your life and drive you even more to succeed.

CHAPTER 7

KEEP TRACK OF YOUR ACHIEVEMENTS

Aside from knowing what to do to achieve your dreams, it is equally important to keep track of them. This is how you can measure your success and there are popular ways to do it.

It is a good idea to start any project with a strategic plan on how to complete it. You have to go back to that plan during the course of the project to see if you are doing things right. It is an important element that will determine if you are still on track.

Once you complete the project, you have to make a summary about its major aspects and how such aspects contribute to reaching your goals. Make sure to write down as many aspects as there are. This is one way to monitor your achievements.

Another method is to write down all the recognition that you received for your achievements. Compile a folder of these notes and keep them. This is not only an effective way of keeping track of all your accomplishments, but it is also a good source of motivation when you feel lost and down.

All the acknowledgements that you have saved up will serve as proof of how great you were with your other projects and how capable you are to take on new challenges. Your compilation can easily become your portfolio, especially if you want to be an expert in your field.

Take an active role in joining community activities, internal committees, company boards, and representative bodies to give yourself the exposure that you needed. These will also add to your experience that can boost the confidence that you need to handle the changes that come with your desire to transform your life.

If you want to maintain a positive mindset, just look at your well-documented achievements. Tell yourself that if you were able to handle them before, you'll be able to handle so much more in the future.

Achievement tracking will keep your capabilities in check. The more capabilities and experiences you know you have, the more confident you will feel that you can turn your life around and be the achiever that you dream to be.

CHAPTER 8

MAKING IT REAL WITH VISUALIZATIONS

When people think about transforming their lives, plans usually include switching jobs, improving their health, building or rebuilding relationships, and boosting their finances, among other thoughts. Although thinking about these things is a good start towards making that change, it would be so much better if you act on these thoughts.

After thinking your plans and priorities through, visualize everything. This might not be easy at first, but you will eventually get used to it the more you do it. Visualization has long been a secret in reaching one's goals, boosting one's confidence, and enjoying life.

You can't change your life as significantly as you'd like unless you change yourself from within. Make plans with a clear mind, so you can easily visualize your dreams the path that you have to take to get to those dreams.

It would be easier to focus on your goals if you visualize them. Create an image of your goals, how you are going to achieve them, and how doing so will affect your life. The stronger your desire to reach your goals, the more chances you will have of taking actions that will contribute to your ultimate success.

How To Achieve Your Goals Through Visualization

Visualizing your goals can be tough at first, but it would be easier if clear your mind and stay in a quiet place. It helps if you stay in a dark room, get rid of all sorts of distractions, like your phone, TV or computer, and choose a comfortable position.

You have to relax. Breathe in, breathe out slowly. Take your mind off your problems. Remove all your self-doubts. Just focus on your breathing.

Close your eyes and savor the feeling of being relaxed. Paint an image in your mind about your goal. You have to be honest and realistic about it. It is not practical to see yourself winning millions in the lottery. You have to be very specific about your vision to really focus on it, such as losing weight or getting a new job. Put in your desire to get to that goal and see yourself finally achieving it. This might take time, but with enough practice, visualization will come easy to you.

When visualizing, what's more important is the goal in itself. During that moment, don't think about the how's and why's related to that goal. You can answer these questions later. Over time, your mastery of visualizing your goals might allow you to set your goals even higher.

Make sure to pick at least one image in your mind's eye every time you visualize. How will it feel to finally lose weight or doing your dream job? How can you tell if you have succeeded? Create an image of the celebration that you'll do once you have reached that goal or the reward that you will give yourself afterwards.

After you have become an expert in visualization, you might be able to do it anywhere, even in a room that is not as quiet or as peaceful as your own room. Just make yourself comfortable and bring all your energy to your breathing. Relax. Start painting that image of finally succeeding, seeing a slimmer you or working in your new office. Take in that joyous feeling of celebrating your success for about 2 seconds. It would be even better if you can hold onto that feeling for up to 15 minutes.

If you become distracted and you can't find your focus, regain your control by reminding yourself of your biggest goals and your strong intent to achieve them. It could be getting your dream job, losing weight, buying a new home, or getting a college degree. No matter what it is, just steer your focus back to that ultimate goal and visualize it.

CHAPTER 9

TO SUM IT ALL UP: MOTIVATION AND ACHIEVING ULTIMATE SUCCESS

Transforming your life starts with determining your dreams and making a definite plan on how to achieve them. Make sure to set a clear and realistic end goal. It has to be achievable within the time frame that you set for it.

With every goal that you achieve, you will feel more and more confident as you continue with your journey in life. It might be a foreign feeling at first, but you will get used to it over time. Boosting your confidence is a good start towards living life with positivity, until it becomes a normal part of your life. This is what you need to change and succeed. Believe in the power of positivity, savor it, live it.

Once you recognize the power of positivity, start visualizing your goals and let them dominate your conscious mind. Visualization will intensify your motivation to succeed and bring you closer to your total transformation. Change your life one step at a time, while staying motivated with every step.

Printed by Libri Plureos GmbH in Hamburg,
Germany